Children first

Growing up in Sweden

THE SWEDISH INSTITUTE

THE SWEDISH INSTITUTE is a public agency entrusted with disseminating knowledge about Sweden abroad and arranging exchanges with other countries in the fields of culture, education, research and other sectors of public life. The Institute supplies a rich array of information material about Sweden. These publications can be obtained directly from the Institute or from Swedish embassies and consulates abroad.

Photographs by Maria Söderberg
Translated by Stephen Croall
Graphic Design by Lisa Jansson/Global Reporting Sweden
Reproduction and printing by Boktryck, Helsingborg 2003
Typeset with Swedish typeface Birka on environmentally-friendly 130 g Munken Lynx, cover 250 g Arctic Silk
Footprints on the inside cover by Tilda Fransson, 9 weeks
Cover photo: Anna, Oda and Disa from Lund
ISBN 91-520-0750-2

CONTENTS

Pippi Longstocking never wants to grow up

"Ugh, I never want to grow up," says Annika to Pippi and Tommy in one of Astrid Lindgren's most widely read and widely translated books about Pippi Longstocking. The trio have just returned from Kurrekurredutt Island and Annika and Tommy have been given generous presents by their passionate, happy-go-lucky friend.

Pippi doesn't want to grow up, either.

"Nothing but corns and minicipal taxes and other boringnesses," she says.

And grownups do indeed seem to have a boring time of it, for the most part. They're always in a hurry and they're always having to read the newspaper or watch the news, and they're almost never overcome with joy at being able to splash around in a warm puddle or lock themselves in a room with their friends.

Under the UN Convention on the Rights of the Child from 1989, which came into force in Sweden the following year, the best interests of the child must always be a primary consideration. And if every decision is to be taken with the best interests of the child in mind, we must decide what in fact represents the child's best interests.

We can do so by adopting a child's perspective on life, by asking the children themselves – as a group or individually – and by turning their own experiences to good account.

From a 'childish' viewpoint, "minicipal taxes and other boringnesses" are part of life to come, and are probably unavoidable. But here and now, there are hostile, prickly bushes on housing estates and poisonous berries beside the playground to contend with, and at school there are fire escapes that are too steep to climb. There are heavy doors that slam shut on your fingers, and, incredibly, no pedestrian crossings outside the school. Worst of all, though, there are parents who are incapable of giving their children the security or love that are as vital to them as the air they breathe and the food they eat.

Looking at life from a child's viewpoint is a valuable exercise, a reminder that children are citizens and active participants in society, both as individuals and as a social group.

Most adults are aware that they have a particular responsibility for children, and most are of course agreed that each and every childhood should be a happy one. This is partly because childhood is a process taking place right now but also because it leaves its mark on us. Childhood is a treasure-trove of memories that call to mind both terrors and magic.

In our day and age, childhood is considered valuable precisely because it provides so much of the basis for a person's subsequent development. Each early experience establishes a framework for the interpretation of new events. Given this understanding, there is of course no excuse for societies and families failing to guarantee each child a good upbringing, full of satisfied needs and respected rights.

A fifth of all inhabitants in Sweden are children, that is people who have not yet turned 18. Some of them believe in the tooth fairy and Santa Claus, others believe in God. Some don't believe in anything at all. Some want to play football or music, others prefer to sit and read. Some are happy at home, others can't wait to get to school.

None of them are entitled to vote at elections, but as children in Sweden they are in fact expected to assert themselves, both in the community and in the family.

Nowadays, many parents, decision-makers and other adults are learning the difficult art of listening to children. The ambition is for Sweden to become a child-friendly society, in accordance with the wishes of the electorate.

In this book, we meet Sara, Felipe and Oda, three typically unusual children in Sweden.

The day Sara's catch fed the whole school

Sara Lestander is a real sleepyhead. Not exactly a clothes freak, she admits. She's not thinking of getting a summer job. Summer holidays are for swimming and lying in the sun. And fishing in the lake of course. You should never ever hit children. Because it's a dreadful thing to do. You should bite them in the ear instead. No, not seriously. But you should ask nicely.

Do you believe in God?
I'm not bothered that much.

What do you do in your spare time?
Simon my neighbour and I, we get up to all kinds of things. I've made some bows, and we shoot arrows.

Is there anything boys are allowed to do that girls aren't allowed to?
Jeez, no! No way!

Will you be taking a summer job?
NOOOO! Summer holidays are for sunbathing and swimming. We usually go fishing and swimming in the lake.

Are you stressed out?
In the mornings, yes. Because I'm such a sleepyhead. Mum sets breakfast for me, then drives Samuel to the day nursery at seven. So I'm left to myself until the school bus arrives.

Laisvall is a community in the municipality of Arjeplog. It is situated on Lake Laisan, 40 km west of Arjeplog and some 800 km north of the Swedish capital, Stockholm. The total population of Laisvall and neighbouring Laisvallby is 326 (2002).

Lapland is an area in northernmost Sweden on the Arctic Circle. It borders on Norway in the west and Finland in the east.

The Sami (previously known as Lapps) are an ethnic and linguistic minority in northern Scandinavia and the Kola Peninsular. There are some 60,000 Sami, of whom around 17,000 live in Sweden, 35,000 in Norway, 5,700 in Finland and 2,000 in Russia.

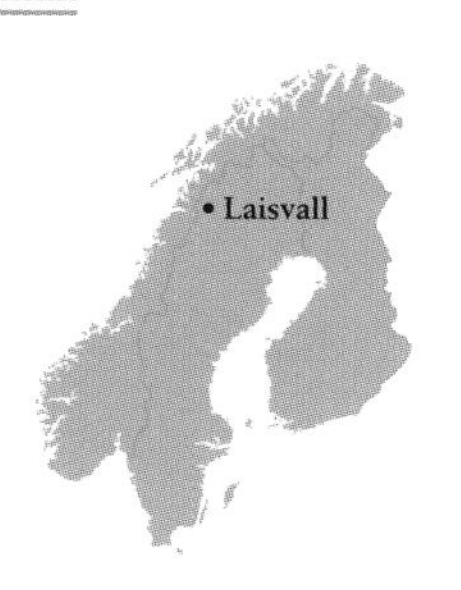

Sara Lestander has been around for almost eleven years now. She has shot a rat and she knows that an elk's heart is big and blue, that codfish have pot bellies and that cockerels are capable of laying eggs, even if they very seldom do. She recognises fox droppings in the mountains and she has captured a lemming without being bitten. Very little frightens her and she seems to cope with most things. If you ask Sara Lestander what her parents won't allow her to do, she'll tell you (wait for it!):

"Inherit grandma's elk-hunting rifle!"

Sara lives in the village of Laisvallby in Swedish Lapland, in the far north where the midnight sun shines on summer nights and where daylight is scarcely visible around Christmas. Her best friend is Simon, who lives in the house opposite. Next door live Sara's paternal grandmother and grandfather.

Just a few hundred metres from Sara's newly-built wooden house lies Lake Laisan. There, you can go fishing in the summer and in winter you can drive a snowscooter across the lake up to the mountains, to the peaks of Niepsurt or Kraja, where the Samis' reindeer rove at dusk and where the ptarmigans cackle at dawn.

As a rule, Sara's life is never dull or humdrum. She has time for plenty of adventures and games. She only has homework about once a week.

"Homework is something you do at school. When you're home you should have fun," she says with total conviction.

Sara is happy with her life on the whole, except on days when it rains. Then she finds things terribly boring – until she realises that she can go over to Simon. They practise with their bows and arrows and do experiments in their own chemistry laboratory. The lab is in Simon's grandmother's house, just across the street, in the old boiler-room.

Sometimes, Sara is happy just to watch TV or read a book. Being alone at home, she says, is actually a relief, as she is then left in peace.

Sara gets to decide quite a lot, she says, both in school and at home. Within the family, matters are settled through discussion and negotiation, says her mother.

"I'm allowed to do most of the things I want," says Sara.

There are only 15 pupils in Sara's school. Eight years ago, there were 51. But the Laisvall lead and zinc mine, which had been operating since the Second World War, was closed down last year. The village has been emptying as jobs disappear.

The remaining 326 residents of Laisvall and Laisvallby are now hoping that the municipality of Arjeplog, to which they belong, will continue to attract car industries from all corners of the world to the largest car testing centre in Europe. In Arjeplog, carmakers test how their vehicles perform on ice and snow. The villagers are also hoping that some of the Norwegians who have bought local property will decide to settle in the area. Otherwise, Laisvall School for pupils aged 7–12 may have to close down. If the number of pupils falls below 13, the local authority may have difficulty keeping it going.

All the pupils at the school know one another. The teachers talk about a family atmosphere there, about how the children look after one another.

It is obvious that the teachers care about the children, too. The pupils have asked for a large trampoline in the schoolyard. And they are pretty sure they will not be disappointed.

About once a month, Sara's class go on excursions into the mountains. They have gone fishing and camping far from home on a number of occasions. They have camped so late in the winter that snow fell on the tents and it was so cold that they had to light a big fire and keep it burning all night.

This autumn, says Sara, the class went to a camp in Norway. They caught so much fish that they had to wheel it home in a wheelbarrow. Sara was particularly lucky.

"Now, listen to this," says Sara as the class sit together in front of their 'activity file', filled with pictures and stories about their travels and outings.

"That codfish was so heavy that at first I thought the hook had caught in the lakebed. It was so big, there was enough of it to feed the whole school."

"There was even some left over," adds Simon.

Not so strange, perhaps. The cod weighed five kilos, and to judge by the photograph inside Sara's school desk, its head was almost as large as hers.

After the cod had been hauled in, their class teacher, Lillemor, seized it in what is known as the 'Lillemor Grip' and killed the fish by breaking its neck.

And that was the end of the cod.

Was this the happiest day of Sara's life?

"I don't know. But it was the happiest day of my happy fishing life," says Sara.

It's Monday morning and the pupils have been travelling for half an hour by bus to get to the Kyrkholm School in Arjeplog for a woodwork lesson.

Mats is the teacher. He operates the electric saw and helps out wherever he is needed.

Sara is building a large wooden box. In time, it will be painted blue and will be used for keeping secret things in. This, she says, is the fifth box she has made in woodwork.

Outside, the April snow gleams. It will soon be melting. But there is still ice on Lake Hornavan, the deepest lake in Sweden. The temperature has risen to 4° C and spring is on the way. In the classroom, the radio is on.

"That's a good song – Daddy, daddy cool," sings Sara.

And then she blurts out as she impatiently screws the lid onto her box:

"I'm really longing for summer. Then I'll be able to go fishing and pick bilberries."

Summer has its advantages in Laisvall.

"If we're hungry, we just go and eat bilberries and then we're not hungry any more."

It would be great if the box could be completed today, or preferably yesterday, judging by Sara's pace of work. Eva-Karin is also making rapid progress. She is carving a Lord of the Rings sword. The pupils often play Harry Potter or the Lord of the Rings. Eva-Karin has been interested in the theatre and role games ever since her third year at school. When she grows up, she wants to act.

Sara is not sure what she wants to do.

"I'll see when I get older," she says. "It's much easier if you have a dream. But you don't have to worry about things like that yet."

Then she brightens up:

"Oh, I remember. I want to be an ice hockey player!"

Sara wants to go on living close to her family when she grows up. Preferably in Laisvall or Laisvallby.

Previous page

Happy hunters. Sara and Grandpa. Sara's grandparents live next door. Just imagine if Sara could inherit her granny's elk rifle one day!

"It's really beautiful around here and there's not much rubbish about," she says. "And the water's clean. Sometimes I just put my hand in the stream and drink."

"You know what I think's a pity? That they had to close the sweet-shop."

The only shops remaining are the food store, which also houses the post office nowadays, and the Sundström brothers' scooter and fishing store.

Nor are there many organised activities, at least not for young people who unlike Sara are not keen on hunting, fishing and camping out. The youth centre is for teenagers only. Eva-Karin is not as interested in outdoor life as the others in Sara's class, and she thinks there's too little to do in Laisvall. But when the class sets out on adventures, there's not much she can do but grin and bear it.

"I go along, most of the time. I'm used to fishing and that kind of thing because my father's a Sami," says Eva-Karin.

When the fourth and fifth years arrive back at their own school, everyone plays rounders in the yard. The young preschool children cycle to and fro on their tricycles, totally unconcerned that they might be upended by someone in the batting side.

Sara describes herself as being 'fairly good' at sports, but in point of fact she seems to be very accomplished. She keeps bashing the ball quite a distance with the rounded bat, beyond the tarmac.

In her spare time, Sara often cycles the four kilometres in to Laisvall to play rounders or bandy. And, like just about everyone else in her class, she plays hockey twice a week at the Laisvall ice-hall, where Simon's father is the coach.

For lunch, it's sausages and mash. The whole school eat together. Ann-Christin is the school cook and today she has baked fresh bread. Simon takes the opportunity to talk about something that has upset him.

"I heard my parents talking about us moving. So I shouted 'No' so they could hear it all the way from my room." Jenny feels the same way.

"I'd tie myself to something if anyone said we were going to move."

What will happen, then, when the time comes for everyone to change schools, when they begin their seventh year in Arjeplog, 40 kilometres away? Will the class stay together?

"Don't know," says Sara.

"Yes, I think so," says Jenny.

At the end of the day the Sundström brothers' little red bus, the one that also delivers the post, arrives to collect the children living in Laisvallby and Adolfström.

Woodwork. Sara's now on to her fifth box. She's going to paint it blue and keep secret things in it. Teacher lends a hand.

When Sara gets home, she says hello to the pet rabbit, Mulle, before going up to her room. Britney Spears hangs on the wall of her blue bedroom, which is cosy and tidy except for the unmade bed. Britney is not exactly her idol – Sara prefers a girl's group called *Atomic Kitten*. She also likes a humorous group called *Pistvakt* as well as *Brandsta City Släckers*, a group of firemen who competed in the Swedish qualifiers for the Eurovision Song Contest.

Because they're good-looking, perhaps?

"Good-looking? No, they're old men!"

Samuel, Sara's younger brother, is six. He plays with a steam-engine in the kitchen during their afternoon snack. After day nursery he usually spends a lot of time driving around on his fast new quadbike. Engines and motor vehicles have to be mastered round here, as it is almost impossible to get up

At last. Dad's come home from work and is making a snack. The snow's sparkling outside. Things look promising.

into the mountains without a snowscooter or a vehicle with four-wheel drive.

While waiting for her father to get home Sara goes round to her grandparents next door. They have opened the garage doors and are sitting catching the sun. Inside, grandma offers Sara a slice of bread from a loaf she has baked and spreads it with home-made marmalade.

Sara's father arrives from work. For the time being he still has a job, working the pumps in the mine. In two weeks' time, when Sara turns eleven, he will find out if he is being kept on in some capacity or whether he will join the ranks of the unemployed. The mine has been closed, and only the clearing-up work remains.

Sara sometimes goes shopping in Skellefteå with her mother, but with her father she always goes into the countryside. Like now, when they are off to the mountains with a scooter and a sledge covered in reindeer skins.

Up on Mount Niepsurt, Sara has prepared a trap to snare grouse. Without a word, Sara and Samuel go off to the next peak to look for animal tracks among the rocks. There are tracks just about everywhere. They find lemming fur – a bird of prey presumably found the lemming. They also find fox, reindeer and hare droppings.

Ptarmigan, white as snow, sit on the mountain rim. They are rounder in shape than doves.

"Ptarmigan are really beautiful," says Sara.

Samuel heads off up the slope, moving carefully so as not to frighten the birds. When he is only a couple of arm's lengths away, they take off and soar into the heavens.

Riding a scooter is like riding a roller coaster at a funfair but better. At the end of a bumpy ride, Sara finds that her mother has arrived home from work – she is a school secretary in Arjeplog. Time for the evening meal.

In the hall, Samuel is feeding Mulle the rabbit, who sits in his cage under the stairs.

"The funny thing about this rabbit is that he likes chocolate," says Samuel, and breaks off a piece to feed his pet with.

"It really eats well," he sighs.

After a while, his mother wonders what's wrong with Mulle. He seems to be having stomach trouble. Phew, what a smell! She lets Mulle out onto the verandah.

Bedtime is approaching but it is still light outside. Sara throws herself onto the couch to watch TV.

Samuel has to go to bed, but he finds all kinds of reasons for not going upstairs, like having another drink and going to the toilet. Life just isn't fair.

Next morning lessons resume in earnest. The pupils are split up into groups. Some of them are placed in the reading room where there are armchairs.

The lesson is Swedish: dictation for class 4, while the fifth years have to learn difficult words on their own. Many words that are self-evident to children in southern Sweden are strange to Sara's class, says Lillemor. Only three of them have ever travelled by train, for instance. The Swedish word *perrong* (platform) sounds like a cake or a pastry. Or could it be something you wear?

There is a kitchen at the back of the classroom, and a table where the pupils can sit and draw or experiment with electricity. All have their own desks. Sara's is tidy, decorated inside with photographs and drawings of a cod, a coalfish and a plaice.

Tomorrow is outdoor recreation day. The class are going to fish through holes in the ice and everyone is to assemble at nine o'clock. Remember to bring along extra socks, knives, plastic bags for your shoes, chocolate and sandwiches for refreshment-time.

But before it's time to go home they are going to have a relaxation session. First, the pupils sing a romantic song.

"I lived for an eternity believing you did not exist," they sing.

Then they lie down on the floor. A taped voice intones:

"Welcome to a journey into the imagination. In your imagination, everything is possible. Everything you wish for can be granted. You're now entering a magic meadow. ... Before you is a rippling stream, all the colours of the rainbow. This is a magic meadow. You can draw strength from it. Nature is magical. There's so much here to learn and so much to discover."

And doesn't Sara know it.

Up and away. In the mountains there's not a soul as far as the eye can see. No litter either. Soon the reindeer will be returning after the winter. Of course Sara never wants to move away from here.

An almost inaccessible kingdom

"To let him [the child] move about freely in this world until he comes into contact with the permanent boundaries of another's right will be the aim of the education of the future. Only then will adults really obtain a deep insight into the souls of children, now an almost inaccessible kingdom."

The above quote is from *The Century of the Child*, a collection of articles about children and child-rearing written by Ellen Key, the radical Swedish author and social activist, and published in Sweden in 1900 (English edition 1909). The book was dedicated to "all those parents who hope to shape the new citizens of a new century."

As Key saw it, human nature was not predetermined. With the right upbringing, future generations would be able to develop into a nobler, more refined type of human being.

Ellen Key argued that childhood was a phase in life with its own conditions and potential. Children, she wrote, were entitled to be surrounded by beauty, in school as well, and she strongly advocated decorating homes in a plain, simple style with light colours. She opposed Christianity's ideal of religious suffering and spoke out in favour of the child's right to develop his or her imagination. According to Key, school should liberate the individual, not cram children's heads with knowledge. Children were to be fostered through freedom and encouragement, and by giving them the opportunity to experience the consequences of their actions.

As it turned out, the 20th century did not become the century of the child in the sense Key had hoped. Yet by the end of the century, the concept of children's rights had become established around the world – not least in Sweden.

A century after Ellen Key first presented her ideas, children as a group are today attracting a great deal of attention in Swedish society. Sweden now has a government minister responsible for children as well as a Children's Ombudsman. Numerous TV and radio programmes focus on life as viewed from a child's perspective. The national curricula for preschool, compulsory school and upper secondary school all specify that education must be child-centred. In addition, the Swedish Riksdag (parliament) has adopted one of the world's first national strategy programmes for the implementation of the UN Convention on the Rights of the Child – a strategy whereby all government decisions concerning children are to be preceded by what is termed a child impact analysis.

Thus Sweden is pursuing a deliberate policy of placing children in the centre. Children and their rights are a focal point today as never before.

Never ever beat a child

"One can indeed see the dawning of an age when the corporal punishment which still takes place in our homes and schools will be regarded just as we today regard the methods of torture practised in earlier, cruder eras."

(From: Ellen Key *The Century of the Child*)

Ellen Key was right in 1900 when she foresaw a new attitude towards corporal punishment. In 1979, a full ten years before the UN General Assembly adopted the Child Convention, Sweden became the first country in the world to outlaw the beating of children.

The ban was unique, not least in that it was based on respect for the child as an individual. The law showed that parents do not own their children – that children are independent individuals with their own rights.

The ban on beating children or punishing them physically was also influential in that it altered people's attitudes towards child rearing in a short space of time. In Sweden today, the accepted view is that a parent should

The **age of criminal responsibility** in Sweden is 15. Children under that age who commit a criminal offence are the responsibility of the social services. From the age of 15 the most usual sanctions for young offenders are fines or care supervised by the social services. Serious offenders will normally be sentenced to secure institutional treatment under the auspices of the National Board of Institutional Care (SiS). Only in exceptional cases may a young person be sent to prison.

Find out more on www.stat-inst.se

never hit a child – under any circumstances. Children who are hit learn to hit others, the argument goes, and it is one that has caused a majority of parents to support the ban on physical punishment.

In the international arena, the law forbidding child beating was controversial at the time of its adoption – and remains so today. Only a dozen or so countries have followed Sweden's example. The issue of child beating still divides societies around the world in their attitude to children's rights.

The competent child – the Swedish view

Over the centuries people have looked upon childhood in different ways. Children were long regarded as unformed little adults who had to be made to adjust to the laborious routine of everyday life by means of coercion, threats and whippings.

In the 20th century, the evolutionary psychological approach to children gained ground in many parts of the world. According to this model, children are shaped by the interaction of environment and biology. Thus they are not biologically predetermined but are formed by the way their needs are met and by how the people around them relate to them as individuals.

Implicit in this understanding of children's needs, and of how children develop, was the concept of children's rights. With the UN Child Convention in place, it is now accepted that children are individuals with specific human rights of their own. They are entitled to health, education, social security, a reasonable living standard, play and leisure. Children are entitled to their own language, to culture and to an identity of their own. Children are entitled to express their opinions and they have the right to be listened to.

And now that these rights have been established by virtually every government and parliament around the world, grownups can no longer view children either as unformed adults or as defenceless packages. Children may be smaller and they may find it much harder to make their voices heard, but they are nonetheless capable individuals. They can speak for themselves – for adults, it is simply a case of knowing how to listen.

In Sweden, too, the way children are viewed has shifted in recent decades from 'the defenceless child with needs' to 'the competent child with rights'. Children are not a different species – they resemble adults both in that they want to master and learn about the world around them and in that they are capable of expressing their own opinions.

But the right of a child to have a say also implies a degree of responsibility and new obligations. In the Swedish public debate on contemporary childhood, it is sometimes argued that children of today are perhaps expected to speak for themselves and to know what is best for them to an inordinate degree. It should not be forgotten that children are not fully matured individuals.

Another question that needs to be asked is why the current emphasis on children's competence happens to coincide with the apparent yearning of many adults nowadays to remain young for as long possible.

One warning heard in the debate is that many parents and adults in Sweden are abdicating from their duty to set a good example to their children and provide them with moral guidance. Perhaps there is some truth in the claim that parents in Sweden are unwilling to grow up and shoulder their responsibility.

On equal terms

"A people's home worthy of the name knows neither privilege nor neglect, neither favour nor disfavour," declared Prime Minister Per Albin Hansson in his historic *Folkhem* speech to the Riksdag in 1928.

Ever since that speech was held, the Social Democrats, the ruling party in Sweden throughout almost the entire post-war period, have sought to realise Per Albin Hansson's vision of a people's home, a society in which everyone found a place by the hearth and no-one was excluded. With the help of social engineering and strong central government, resources were to be distributed equitably and classes were to be levelled.

A recipe for success, it was felt, was to start with the country's young and develop a social welfare policy that embraced all children. Universal child benefit, the same for all children, a nine-year compulsory school and free dental and medical care for all children were among the reforms introduced in the spirit of the *folkhem*.

Not all children enjoy the support of parents capable of giving them what they need to develop. Consequently, the post-war community builders agreed, universal welfare policies must be combined with support for children at risk.

The golden age of the Swedish welfare model is sometimes said to have passed. The *folkhem* ideal is dead and the welfare society is being dismantled, or so many commentators declared in the debate that followed the crisis years of the 1990s, when countless children paid a heavy price for extensive cuts in the public sector.

Some observers also claim to have detected a political sea change on the horizon, coming from the right and paving the way for greater class distinctions and thus greater differences in children's social circumstances.

In educational policy in Sweden, there are clear differences between the approaches advocated by the various political parties represented in the Riksdag. The centre-right, in particular, advocates 'freedom of choice' and private educational alternatives, while the Social Democrats and their allies place greater emphasis on 'a school for all'.

Nevertheless, the vision of a social security net around children protecting them from harm is, it would seem, still alive in Sweden. There appears to be a consensus on the need to maintain general welfare policies aimed at ensuring that children from different social backgrounds enjoy the same kinds of conditions and starts in life.

Child allowances were introduced in 1947 with the aim of reducing differences in the standard of living between people with and without children. The allowance is paid for all children in Sweden up to the age of 16.

Child health-care centres (BVCs) offer advice and guidance during the first 7 years of a child's life. Contact with the BVC is voluntary for parents, but most visit the centre regularly after the child is born. Having previously concentrated on issues such as breastfeeding and sleeping problems, physical checkups and child vaccinations, the centres have recently begun to provide families with psychosocial support as well.

Sweden is ranked second (after Norway) on the **United Nations' Human Development Index**, a composite index which measures average achievement in three basic dimensions of human development: a long and healthy life, knowledge, and a decent standard of living.

Policies in the best interests of the child

In one sense, present-day child policy in Sweden goes further than the *folkhem* ideal in its determination to put the people's house in order. Its express goal is to make all areas of Swedish society child-friendly and to ensure that all government decisions are informed by a children's perspective.

Since 1993, Sweden has had a Children's Ombudsman (BO), whose task is to safeguard children's rights and interests and to monitor national compliance with the UN Child Convention. The Swedish cabinet also includes a minister for children and the family.

In 1999, the Riksdag adopted a national strategy for implementing the UN Convention on the Rights of the Child. The aim of this strategy is to ensure that the Convention and the principle of acting in the child's best interests are properly observed in all policy decisions concerning children.

This national strategy is important and unique in many respects. Sweden, for instance, is one of the first countries to work systematically with a children's perspective in this way. The strategy also heralds some truly profound changes in the decision-making process. It stipulates that child impact analyses must be performed in connection with all central government decisions concerning children.

This means that a children's perspective is to be applied, for instance, when drawing up the national budget, when drafting legislation concerning

---

Since 1993 children and young people in Sweden have had an Ombudsman of their own. The main task of the **Children's Ombudsman** (BO) is to safeguard the rights and interests of children and young people in society as laid down in the UN Convention on the Rights of the Child.

Find out more on www.bo.se

Child impact analyses must now be carried out in connection with all central government decisions which affect children. A child impact analysis shall determine what the best interests of the child are by looking at how children would be affected short-term and longterm by a particular decision, and by listening to children's own views.

children and when discussing transportation and the planning of physical environments. A children's perspective should also be incorporated into the terms of reference of government commissions of inquiry.

But the UN Child Convention has yet to become a generally accepted tool in central government decisions. Furthermore, most decisions concerning children are made not by central government but by local and county councils. For the time being, neither are required to provide child impact analyses. Municipal autonomy is extensive in Sweden and central government cannot impose such a requirement on local authorities without careful consideration.

Nevertheless, government child policy specifically aims to bring the issue of a children's perspective onto the local and regional agenda, and many local authorities have already integrated child impact analyses into their activities.

Thus, although there is still far to go, it can be said that the UN Child Convention and the child's perspective are being taken seriously by decision-makers in Sweden today.

The child's say

Children may not be entitled to vote at elections until they are eighteen, but they still have the right to express their opinion and to have it respected.

The trend in Sweden is increasingly moving towards viewing children as individuals and as citizens worthy of respect. One sign of this is the fact that a proposal to lower the voting age in local council elections from 18 to 16 has been discussed at the initiative of the National Board for Youth Affairs. Another issue under discussion is whether to grant children what is called civil rights of proposal at local level, which would mean local and county councils allowing all citizens to bring motions before council meetings.

The idea behind these initiatives has often been to revitalise democracy. But the proposal to lower the voting age may also offer a solution to the difficult question of how society is to listen to children as a group in the community.

Society's obligation to listen to individual children is an easier problem to solve. A number of provisions to regulate this obligation are already in place. In cases where the social services investigate and report on individual children in difficulties, the Social Services Act contains a crucial paragraph stating that the best interests of the child are to take precedence. Children are also allowed to have their say in cases concerning them, i.e. to express an opinion and to have it respected. Other occasions on which society is required by law to give children their say is when dealing with cases under the Parental Code, with adoption cases and with those coming under the Care of Young Persons (Special Provisions) Act.

NGVE
YEK
REVIEW

Spårvägen
SINCE 1978

Felipe's a midfielder, like Zidane

Spanish is the language of the heart, but Felipe Ramirez Ghiglione never wants to move to Chile. He's got nine marks against his name on the blackboard and 100 football shirts. He's good at maths, can do jumps on his bike and is fascinated by the crows nesting outside his window. Felipe hurts his foot one day. For a midfielder with the summer holidays just around the corner, that's pretty unfortunate!

What are you going to do this summer?
Play with my friends all day. And then we're going to Legoland in Denmark with my dad and some friends.

Do you like it in Skarpnäck?
Very much! I've got thousands of friends here. I know everyone, even if I don't know their names.

Do you and Carla miss your dad?
Yes. Too much, sometimes.

Are you afraid of anyone?
Of people that drink a lot and people who snatch children.

Are you nervous when you're going to play a match?
No, I've played so many matches before.

In 2000 there were 10450 people living in Skarpnäck. Twenty percent of them were under 19 years of age. There are 4,300 homes in the area, most of them flats built since 1981.

Felipe Ramirez Ghiglione – surely a name to suit a top professional footballer. And a football star, just like Zinedine Zidane, is precisely what nine-year-old Felipe wants to be when he grows up.

Felipe is a broad-shouldered midfielder who trains and plays matches several times a week.

Bosse and Hasse are the team coaches. They shout encouragement and criticism at the players by turns.

"Head the ball! There isn't a football player anywhere who'd duck a ball like that," they shout in their broad Stockholm accents.

Felipe's younger sister, Carla, stood on the balcony in the afternoon singing an Indian song to stop the rain but it hasn't helped. Felipe is having to play football in an ice-cold downpour. A substitute today, he stands, wet through, on the touchline of his team's dirt-grey home pitch in Skarpnäck on the outskirts of Stockholm. When his mother offers him a pair of tracksuit bottoms, he rejects them immediately, although all the other boys have already donned them over their shorts.

Nor is he the least bit interested in a drink of water.

This is a match.

Pierina, Felipe's mother, is the only parent on the sidelines to make her voice heard.

"*Heja, heja*," she shouts, forgetting that Felipe had begged her at home not to get so involved in the game in future. She hugs little sister Carla – both mother and daughter fit inside a giant plastic raincoat. Carla peers out. Grandma Amantina and Grandpa Juan are also at the match, with umbrellas, as is Felipe's father, Juan Alfonso.

When the final whistle goes with the match drawn 1-1, Felipe's foot is hurting badly. Fortunately, he doesn't have to walk home – he gets a lift with his father.

But Juan Alfonso doesn't go with his son up to the flat because he and Pierina are divorced. Grandma goes with them, however, to help Pierina cook the evening meal. Tonight, Pierina is putting together a giant home-

made pizza with tomato, Parma ham and plenty of mozzarella cheese.

"You thought dad was the only one who could make pizza!" she says to Carla and Felipe, who are sitting contentedly at the round table. For a while now, Pierina has had the feeling that the children think the divorce was her fault. She sometimes gets upset when Felipe describes how his father does this or that at his flat:

"You're always saying things are better at dad's place!"

But Carla objects:

"When he's at dad's place he says things are better here!"

Since the divorce, Felipe and Carla have gone on living with Pierina in their old home – a light, airy flat with a balcony.

Juan Alfonso works as an accountant at Ericsson and lives alone in a small flat just a stop away from the children on the underground. Once he finds a flat in Skarpnäck, the children will be living with him every second week. His parents live in Skarpnäck, just a few blocks from their grandchildren. Pierina's parents are both dead; her father died in Chile last autumn.

Last summer, Juan Alfonso took the whole family to Italy. Pierina went along even though she and Juan had divorced only 18 months previously. The children enjoyed Italy. Felipe got to see a match between Parma and Genoa and he and Carla played with the children of a German family, speaking English.

"I ate hamburgers every day!" says Felipe. But hamburgers and football did not occupy all their time. The family also visited the Vatican on several occasions. Perhaps because one or other of them believes in God?

"If my brother does, I do, too," says Carla.

"I'd rather play with my friends than waste time in places like that," says Felipe.

According to the Swedish national curriculum for the preschool, children who speak another language than Swedish at home should be helped to develop both languages. Compulsory-school pupils have the right to **mother-tongue tuition** and to help with other school subjects in their mother tongue if necessary.

Six percent of 0 to 17-year-olds in Sweden were born outside the country, while 18%, although born in Sweden, have at least one foreign parent. Children of entirely or partly **foreign parentage** account for nearly a quarter (24%) of Sweden's children.

Carla thinks it's far too boring in church.

"You have to be quiet. You can almost never shout," she says.

She adds: "Me and Felipe don't want to watch Pippi Longstocking and stuff like that. We want to see a bit more action."

"Pippi's boring," says Felipe.

"I used to watch her all the time!" exclaims their mother, hunting for something in one of the kitchen cupboards.

"I don't understand how she can have plaits like that," says Carla.

Both Felipe and Carla miss having their father with them – "sometimes too much," as they put it. But he phones every morning, he goes to Felipe's matches and sometimes he does things together with the children, like going with Felipe to away matches or taking them on outings. Every other weekend, Carla and Felipe sleep at their grandparents' flat, where they also meet their father.

The divorce was not without its problems, says Pierina, but she feels it's important not to be negative about the other partner in front of the children.

Juan Alfonso and Pierina share custody of the children. Despite the couple's wish to ensure that the children did not suffer as a result of the divorce, Pierina feels that Felipe in particular has been upset. Pierina, Felipe and Carla meet a woman from the social services once a week to talk through the divorce.

Pierina and Juan Alfonso came to Sweden from Chile as political refugees in 1983. Felipe and Carla, who were both born in Sweden, have been to Chile on visits a number of times, most recently a couple of years ago. But they're not looking forward to going back there, having developed a hatred of all the jabs and vaccinations that are required for the trip. On the other hand, Pablo lives in Chile – a cousin who is 25 years old and really tall.

"Pablo's the baddest cousin," says Felipe admiringly.

Skarpnäck is the final station on one of the underground lines and even if the suburb is well-planned it has a reputation for not exactly being the safest place on earth. Stockholm is a segregated city and in many suburbs with a high concentration of immigrants unemployment has been high, which has led to social problems.

"There used to be lots of Poles living here," says Pierina. "Now it's more mixed. There are a lot of Finnish Roma, and lots of Turks and Latin Americans, most of them from Chile."

The family has plenty of Chilean friends in the area. Their cousins come to visit almost every Sunday.

Previous page

In the mouth of the whale. Felipe and Dad do things together, like going on excursions. When Dad gets a flat nearby the children will be able to stay with him.

Much of what Pierina is anxious to pass on to her children comes from her earlier life in Viña del Mar. This includes the enjoyment of getting together with friends and acquaintances.

"We drank and chatted, we went round to the neighbours, and they gave us drinks or coffee. People always offered you something," says Pierina.

Other aspects of life in Chile were less pleasant. Hitting the children was almost routine procedure, says Pierina. Not to injure them, but to teach them to behave. On the other hand, much has changed over the years – nowadays children's rights are officially recognised in Chile.

"In Sweden, children take advantage of being allowed to say whatever they like. They have the support of the social services and the police and the people in the street. So I'm thinking, if the children have their rights, we adults have ours. What are we supposed to say if they don't listen, however much you try? If they refuse to say, 'I can help you'?

"I don't hit my children but I shake them and plonk them down on a chair and have a serious talk with them. I insist they look me in the eye and I ask them, 'Why do you do that?'"

Both Felipe and Carla have been brought up to respect others at all times.

"Respect is tremendously important – you only get it from others if you show it yourself," says Pierina.

Felipe sits quietly on his chair throughout the meal, although his foot hurts. It just might be a sprained ankle.

"Felipe's got a hundred football shirts," says Carla, which reminds her brother that the children have been given a note at school about another football training camp in the summer.

"What does it cost? I don't know if I can afford it," says Pierina, who has a disability pension. She has a muscular disease that often causes her considerable pain. For Felipe, this means that his mother is at home more than most other mothers in Sweden, who are usually out working during the day. And while the children are in school, Pierina looks after the home. It's a tough job for someone who is in pain and has difficulty finding enough energy.

"Carla often gets up at weekends to fix breakfast for me and Felipe," says Pierina.

"I want Carla and Felipe to enjoy their childhood and not have to shoulder too much responsibility," she adds.

But Carla wants to help and does so all the same.

Planning and preparation are important for Pierina as she has to make every penny count. Her social insurance money is not enough to live on,

Fairy tales. On Fridays it's home-language class. This week they're doing fairy tales. In Spanish, of course.

but she gets by with the help of her housing benefit, maintenance payments from Juan Alfonso, child benefit and help from friends and relations.

Felipe is supposed to be at school at ten past eight every morning.

"I'm never late," he says. "I only turned up late once and then I was given a note to take home."

That's not fair, in Felipe's opinion.

"Our teacher sometimes gets in five or ten minutes late. Then he tells us he was up until two in the morning. But in that case, why does he mark it on the blackboard when we do something wrong?"

Felipe himself has nine marks against his name, which means 45 minutes' detention. This is less than some in the class, but more than others.

You get a mark against your name if you chatter too much, and Felipe often does – at least in school.

Felipe's classroom has a corner sofa where the children can sit and read. One wall is hung with flags that the children have made – each was asked

Happy here. Felipe knows everyone in the building and all his friends live close by.

to draw the flag of his or her native country. There are seven Swedish flags, three from Iran, three from Chile and one each from Argentina, China, Colombia, Gambia, Iraq, the Philippines and Vietnam.

Felipe is good at maths and at the moment he's thinking very hard while twisting his pen between his fingers. He can do sums in his head and he has made good progress in his maths book.

Felipe's class has first-year, second-year and third-year pupils. In all, 22 children are sitting round four large tables. They work with different things depending on what year they are in.

The teacher wanders around amongst the children. His T-shirt carries the message 'Listen to Bob Marley'. Carla says Felipe's class teacher Ante has 'the wickedest haircut'. His hair stands straight up, like a hedgehog.

"You still haven't done anything. Let's see some action," says Ante, urging on one of the pupils.

Suzanne, a remedial teacher and work team leader, is helping one of the girls, while Eddie, a second-year pupil who supports Hammarby, one of Stockholm's top football teams, is so tired he can hardly think straight. He played two matches yesterday. Won one and lost the other, and strained a finger into the bargain. Now he fidgets in his chair and longs for the lesson to end.

After lunch, the pupils rinse their plates. They spend the break skipping and playing ball, tag and cops and robbers. As many as a dozen balls bounce around on the warm tarmac.

At ten past twelve, the bell rings. The first-year and second-year pupils in the class have to go in and present themselves to Ante, and are then allowed to go home or to the recreation centre, which is on the school premises.

The third-year children, however, stay on and are given a Swedish test. Ante reads out the task before them this afternoon.

"Write a letter to a relative you like. Don't forget capital letters and full stops. Write as nicely as you can."

"I'm writing one to my make-believe brother," says Peter.

"Do you eat pens, Felipe?" wonders Ante when Felipe can't find anything to write with.

One of the boys is chattering away. He has finished early after writing a long letter. Ante has already had to tell him off a number of times.

"OK, out you go."

"No."

"Yes."

Ante gives him another chance and the lesson goes on as before. But after another ten minutes or so Ante has had enough of the chatter.

"Thank you and goodbye!" he says, demonstratively opening the door to the corridor.

Sandwiches and milk with cornflakes are on a trolley in the classroom. It's the mid-afternoon snack for those children – like Felipe – who attend the after-school recreation centre in one of the school classrooms. The noise level is high in the room and the recreation leaders seem to talk more with one another than with the children.

Felipe and Azar eat up and leave. They would have preferred to play soccer this afternoon but can't find a football and decide to play basketball instead.

They are definitely not anxious to swap balls with some girls who are playing basketball with a football nearby. The girls don't care, either, throwing their football around and netting time and again.

"You didn't give me a kiss," says Pierina when Felipe sits down for a breather after a long working day, having climbed the stairs to the flat with his rucksack on his back.

"Sorry," says Felipe and kisses his mother on the cheek.

Carla, back from school, goes to change, and now she and Felipe look out over the street from the balcony.

Close by, a giant tree sways in the wind. Crows have built large nests in the branches out of twigs and sticks.

Felipe likes to stand here watching how the crows feed their young, and sometimes when the wind is really strong he manages to catch a branch as the tree bends in towards the balcony.

Today, however, there is only a light breeze. One of the neighbours can be heard playing Oriental music, a woman's wailing voice fills the whole lane of 1980s housing, and below a plump cat minces along the pathway. Another neighbour puts on a hip-hop record and turns the volume up high.

Felipe goes off for a bike ride but things don't always work the way they are meant to. Felipe flies off his mountainbike, crash-lands and cuts his hands, elbows and thigh.

Carla fetches green leaves to place on the cuts, but when Pierina goes to help Felipe to clean his wounds in the kitchen he becomes impatient.

"I can do it myself, OK?" he says, annoyed by the pain.

"Don't talk to me like that!" says Pierina sharply.

Carla dusts off Felipe's tracksuit.

Mustn't Felipe have a tetanus injection now, when there's gravel in the cuts?

"No, I hate jabs."

"Felipe, what if you had to go to war?" says Pierina.

Carla disappears into her mother's bedroom and comes back with her arm in an elastic stocking, like a bandage.

"I've been at war with Felipe," she says with a giggle.

Carla is wearing a new watch she was given for her birthday, glinting silver and all the colours of the rainbow. Felipe is waiting for his birthday present, which he himself helped choose.

"I'd like to wear my black sweatshirt when we go out bowling. Can I get it by then?" asks Felipe, who is keen to have clothes of the right sporty type with the right label.

Carla is less demanding, says Pierina. She doesn't care whether the clothes come from the flea-market or the second-hand shop. Pierina doesn't want the children to have too many possessions.

"I want them to have lots of feelings and to express lots of feelings," she says. "Feelings are the most important thing in life, and respect."

Night is drawing in. Only two weeks until the summer holidays. Carla is playing with a whoopy cushion. Felipe is playing 'Who Wants to be a Millionaire?' on the Internet.

His foot is almost back to normal. The cuts from the bicycle accident will also heal soon. Both mum and Carla actually did quite a good job on them.

There just might be more football ahead this summer.

A school for all

In Sweden, as in many other countries, the state displayed an early interest in the education of children and young people. Like early infant crèches, the state-run schools established in the 19th century were largely a relief project for looking after poor children while the parents worked. With the advent of urbanisation and industrialism, it had become obvious that children without any form of supervision, who simply wandered about the streets, had to be given care.

But even as early as 1842 when the first elementary schools were established, a nurturing dimension was involved – school was to foster citizens and labour.

Around the turn of the last century, calls were heard for school education to be made available to all children, not just those of limited means. And with the subsequent arrival of the *folkhem* – the people's home or welfare society – Swedish schools were perceived as a place where children from different backgrounds were to meet on equal terms. From the outset, therefore, Swedish schools have had other concerns besides the imparting of knowledge.

Today's Swedish school system dates from 1962. It prescribes nine years

The Swedish school system is made up of compulsory and non-compulsory elements. Nine years of schooling between the ages of 7 and 16 are compulsory for all children. Non-compulsory schooling includes 3 hours a day free preschool for children aged 4 to 6 and the post-16 upper secondary school. Almost all compulsory-school students go on directly to 3 years of study at upper secondary school. All education in the school system is free. There is usually no charge for teaching materials, school meals, health services and transport.

See www.skolverket.se for further information

of compulsory schooling, usually beginning at the age of seven, followed by a three-year upper secondary school that is voluntary but which in practice most pupils attend.

As the name implies, children have to attend compulsory school. But they also have a legal right to schooling – to an education that is of an 'equivalent' standard irrespective of gender, place of residence and social and economic circumstances. Children with disabilities, too, are entitled to an equivalent education. School also has a special responsibility for helping children who are unable to achieve the specified educational goals.

Inquiring minds and a questioning attitude

People often say that the relationship between teachers and pupils in Sweden is a familiar and democratic one, or at least evenly balanced. Teachers do not enjoy unquestioned authority but must capture the hearts and minds of their pupils – they acquire authority by virtue of their knowledge and their personal qualities.

Schoolchildren in Sweden often appear inquisitive and independent compared with children in many other countries. The prime reason for this is probably that children are taught from an early age to question things, and Swedish schools seek to encourage reflection and critical thinking. In the spirit of the UN Child Convention, Swedish children are encouraged to express their opinions and to stand up for their rights. Independence rather than obedience is widely considered a desirable quality in children.

Over the past decade, not least due to the knowledge explosion and the emergence of the Internet, the idea that schools can provide pupils with an all-round education from behind the teacher's desk has had to be abandoned. Pupils have increasingly learnt how to seek out the knowledge they need themselves. They learn how to learn – to a great extent, they conduct research and work thematically, focusing on a particular subject in groups or in projects. Teachers try to get away from the traditional division of subject areas by collaborating with one another.

However, basing tuition on the inquiring mind of the pupil places considerable demands on the teacher's own level of knowledge and educational skills. If teachers are unable to actively involve their pupils, the concept of self-instruction can easily founder.

Democratic competence

Swedish school education has undergone some profound changes in recent years. The media have tended to describe school education in terms of a 'crisis area'. Classrooms are rowdy, the media say, teachers have given up and pupils, especially girls, are having to listen to four-letter words flying about the place every day.

There are doubtless a number of reasons why many schools are in such a critical state, foremost among them, perhaps, being a lack of resources following the public sector cuts of the 1990s. The cuts led to an increase in the size of preschool groups and a decline in teacher-pupil ratios in schools.

In 1989 responsibility for the provision of schooling transferred from the state to the municipalities. The state continues to exercise control over both compulsory and upper secondary education, however, by monitoring developments and establishing frameworks in the form of legislation, national curricula and syllabuses.

Swedish pupils compare very well with pupils in other countries in terms of academic performance. Nonetheless, almost ten per cent of those who complete their compulsory education lack passes in one of the core school subjects, Swedish, English and mathematics.

PISA (Programme for International Student Assessment) is a new 3-yearly OECD survey of the knowledge and skills of 15-year-olds in the world's 32 principal industrialised countries. It looks at student performance in reading and in mathematical and scientific literacy. It is interesting to note that Sweden had the second lowest variation in results between schools. This suggests that the Swedish school system does not segregate and that performance is not determined by which school a child attends. The PISA analyses also reveal that a child's social background has less influence on his or her school performance in Sweden than in most countries.

Swedish schools shall impart knowledge, but they also have a **caring function**. Lunches which are free of charge and in which all participate are an important ingredient in the ambition to address the individual as a whole.

Accordingly, many opposition politicians argue that schools must provide children with 'hard' knowledge that is quantifiable and which can be assessed and graded at an early stage. As things stand, Swedish pupils are not given grades until their eighth year. This is because it is thought that until their early teens children are not mature enough to appreciate that the grades represent an assessment of their academic progress and not of their personal qualities.

The most dramatic change in the Swedish educational system has been the arrival of numerous independent compulsory and upper secondary schools as the result of a reform introduced in the 1990s.

Independent schools are not private in the usual sense, as they are not allowed to charge school fees. The solution in Sweden has been to endow private alternatives with municipal grants. The schools are financed 'per child' in accordance with complicated rules concerning what kinds of resources are needed for different children with different needs.

One outcome of the independent school reform is that parents nowadays have a far greater say in their children's education. Pupils can, in consultation with their parents, choose from among a wide range of compulsory and upper secondary schools such as Muslim or arts-oriented schools or ones specialising in IT.

The reform has been criticised on the grounds that it could lead to a more segregated society, as the children of parents who for one reason or another are unable to involve themselves actively in the choice of a school tend to remain in municipal schools. This, it is feared, might lead to a decline in municipal school standards.

With the arrival of a growing number of independent schools, too, the importance of school as a social 'cement' uniting different groups in the community is no longer emphasised in the same way. Consequently, fears have been expressed in some quarters that school education might develop from being a public affair for all into a private one.

The fact remains, however, that the laws that govern the activities of both independent and municipal schools still emphasise the school's fostering role. School should be a place where people from different backgrounds meet and mix. Schools should promote what is termed democratic competence among children and young people, regardless of whether they are municipally run or not. With the school's help, each pupil is to develop into an independent individual who respects and makes allowances for dissenting views.

The Education Act and the various national curricula specify a 'community of values' for school education in Sweden and define the principles that are to inform all school activities. These are the inviolability of human life, freedom and privacy of the individual, gender equality between women and men, and solidarity with the weak and vulnerable.

Zero tolerance on bullying

A demand that is often heard in the media is that schools must step up their efforts to combat bullying. In recent years, several cases of severe assault have occurred in schoolyards, and five per cent of all schoolchildren aged 10-12 say they are bullied at least once a week. Several reports indicate that bullying is on the increase.

Nevertheless, a marked change in attitude has occurred throughout Swedish society – bullying is no longer accepted as a 'necessary evil' or an inevitable part of growing up. Both the Education Act and the national curricula contain strict rules specifying 'zero tolerance' on bullying and abusive treatment. And most schools have drawn up their own action plans for combating bullying.

Parents and pupils are also more inclined nowadays to report violence and harassment to the authorities. Local authorities are legally responsible for tackling bullying, and in a couple of cases pupils have sued them for damages.

Proportion of children of different ages in Swedish childcare (preschool and school-age childcare) in 2000.

1 year	42%
2	78%
3	82%
4	86%
5	88%
6–9	66%
10–12	7%

After a birth or adoption parents are entitled to share a total of 480 days' leave from work in receipt of **parental benefit**. For the first 390 days this usually corresponds to around 80% of the parent's salary; for the remainder of the period they receive 60 kronor per day. Sixty days are specifically earmarked for each parent, the remainder may be shared between them or used by one parent only, as they wish.

The **preschool fee ceiling** means that parents pay no more than 3% of their income to have their children at a day nursery. A smaller fee is charged for the second and third child.

All children aged 6–12 are entitled to supervised care outside school hours – mostly after school, when they can enjoy themselves while waiting for their parents to come home from work. These activities are often integrated into schools, with staff dividing their time between the two, and they often share the same premises. Like preschools, **childcare programmes for school-age children** are a part of the educational system, subject to a national curriculum and supplementing the work of the school.

Some Swedish preschools provide special training in **gender equality**, as studies have shown that boys often receive more attention than girls and are allowed to talk without interruption longer than girls.

Preschool fun – a right

The inviolability of human life, individual freedom and privacy, gender equality between girls and boys – the same community of values as applies in schools also applies in the Swedish preschool.

Preschool education is officially about the right of both mothers and fathers to combine parenthood with a professional life outside the home. For the past few decades, the proportion of women in Sweden who go out to work has been very high. The welfare society and the women's movement have been closely allied since the 1930s. Women, fighting for the right to combine gainful employment with childbearing, have constantly demanded reasonably-priced childcare facilities of good quality. And this has to a large extent been achieved.

Sweden has a very generous parental leave scheme and extensive childcare facilities. Swedish local authorities are obliged to provide a childcare place for every child from the age of 12 months whose parents are out at

work or studying. Three out of four children aged 1–5 were registered in childcare in the autumn of 2000. Since 2002 virtually all Swedish local authorities have introduced a fee ceiling on childcare and they are obliged to offer all four to six-year-olds a place in a preschool class to prepare for compulsory school, which usually starts at the age of seven.

There is much to suggest that most Swedish parents feel their children are happy and develop well at such facilities. What started out as a right for working parents is today viewed equally as a basic right for the young children themselves, despite the fact that it is not compulsory. Accordingly, the children of the unemployed, too, are entitled to at least three hours a day in childcare, regardless of the fact that their parents may be at home and in a position to look after them.

The availability of good, cheap preschool facilities means children get a special kind of early childhood. In contemporary Sweden, professional staff and parents divide care of the children between them – having children is not entirely a private affair. School and childcare are supposed to supplement the home environment and compensate for any failings there. Preschool staff are required to raise the alarm if they suspect that children are being maltreated, if something is going on outside the bounds of normality.

Swedish preschools are a part of the educational system in that they operate under a national preschool curriculum which stipulates that they are to prepare children for 'lifelong learning'. Teachers and staff try to see the whole child. This means that the staff strive to keep the child's entire situation and environment in mind, and also that both preschool and recreational childcare for school-age children have an important caring role to play.

While preschools have an educational task, the idea is not for them to become a kind of 'mini-school' where the child's performance is assessed or measured. The educational aspect refers to children learning through everything they do and experience, from nappy changes to walks in the forest.

Care and supervision, in other words, are to be combined with interest and curiosity and the will to learn. In this respect, games fill an important function. Games are to be played for their own sake, because they are fun, but also because children learn through playing.

Some are less visible than others

All children in Sweden are entitled to grow up under conditions that are conducive to their well-being. This is a basic premise laid down in many of the laws and regulations concerning children and young people in Sweden, including the Education Act, the Social Services Act and the Care of Young Persons (Special Provisions) Act.

The vast majority of Swedish children enjoy decent circumstances. Most live in warm, spacious, modern flats and are able to cope with school. The great majority of children and young people in Sweden never need to feel afraid of going out.

But despite laws and policy aims, there are considerable differences in the circumstances that children live under during their formative years. There are children whose relationships with their parents and step-parents are poor and who are rejected or find it difficult to keep up at school.

These children labour under a double burden. Often, it is the ones from deprived backgrounds who suffer from sleep problems and stress and who feel insecure in their home environments. Many of the children trapped by relative poverty have single parents or parents who were born in another country.

In short, there are cracks in the Swedish welfare structure that society has been unable to fill. Or, to put it more plainly, there are still children who are victims of social injustice.

Children with disabilities

Special efforts are made in Sweden to even out the difference between the conditions under which people with disabilities live and those of others. Children with disabilities of whatever kind have the same needs as other children and young people – but they also require more support.

One of the goals of the Social Services Act and the Act on Support and Service for Persons with Certain Functional Impairments (LSS) is to compensate for disabilities. Government policy seeks to assure children with disabilities of the means to live their lives on equal terms – both during childhood and later.

For a long time, children with disabilities were locked away in homes and institutions and excluded from community life. But at the end of the 1960s, the disability movement grew strong and managed to persuade policy-mak-

The government-appointed **Disability Ombudsman (HO)** monitors the rights and interests of people with disabilities. The objective is for people with disabilities to be able to participate fully in the life of the community and live on the same terms as others. Its operations are based on the UN Standard Rules on the Equalization of Opportunities for Persons with Disabilities from 1993.

Find out more at www.ho.se.

ers that disabled citizens have the right to participate. Integration, not least in schools, became an important goal.

There is a public and political consensus in Sweden that children with disabilities should receive the kind of service and support that enables them to attend ordinary compulsory schools and upper secondary schools. Yet despite extensive efforts to achieve this goal, statistics from the Disability Ombudsman show that half of the country's schools have still not adapted their premises to accommodate pupils with impaired mobility. A great number of these pupils cannot even get through the doors of their nearest school – quite simply because the school has made no allowance for children in wheelchairs.

An alternative school form, primarily for children with intellectual impairments or autism who are deemed incapable of achieving the regular educational goals at compulsory school level, is the special-needs school. In principle, it is up to the parents to decide whether they want their children to attend a special-needs school or an ordinary school.

Most pupils with disabilities go on to upper secondary after compulsory school. The majority of them attend ordinary schools, but special-needs upper secondary schooling is available for those who are either deaf or have impaired hearing. There are also national upper secondary schools for pupils with impaired mobility, in Göteborg, Kristianstad, Stockholm and Umeå.

Children with disabilities naturally have the right not to be subjected to discrimination. But many do not get a fair start in life. Access to special-needs schooling has declined since the 1990s,and many children with disabilities are having to wait a long time before their needs can be met.

Children with disabilities are entitled to special technical aids in school and teaching aids such as easily-read texts, talking books and books in Braille. Yet the Children's Ombudsman has found that many schools lack technical aids for children with disabilities. One child in three with impaired mobility and one in four with impaired vision or DAMP/ADHD Syndrome lack the requisite technical aids, according to the Ombudsman's report. This applies in particular to girls, whose needs are receiving less attention despite the fact that they are no different from boys'. This underlines the fact that girls are still less visible in Swedish society than boys, notwithstanding the widespread awareness of the problem.

Child poverty

Sweden is a rich industrial nation with an inclusive welfare system and a high standard of living. Some ninety percent of children have their own room, live in families with a car and have a computer in the home.

Nonetheless, a government report on welfare trends in the 1990s (*Welfare in Sweden: A Balance Sheet for the 1990s*) found an increase in the proportion of children living in households with – by Swedish standards – scant economic resources. The children of blue-collar workers, single parents and people born abroad tended to be worse off than others, the report showed.

The Swedish Save the Children organisation reached similar conclusions. They found that almost one child in four with a foreign background compared with one in ten others is living in relative poverty, i.e. in a family that has a low income or is dependent on social security. The organisation noted both an increase in the number of children living in economic straits and a widening gap between different municipal areas in terms of children's circumstances. Child poverty was accelerating in large urban centres in particular.

Depopulation is a problem which afflicts rural Sweden and which obstructs the development of services and other opportunities for the local population. The greatest threat in urban areas is segregation, which gives rise to social problems.

Read more about how children and their families have fared in Sweden in recent years in *Welfare in Sweden: The Balance Sheet for the 1990s*, ed. Joakim Palme. Swedish Ministry of Health and Social Affairs, Stockholm 2002.

See www.rb.se for information about **Swedish Save the Children**.

Poor families in Sweden are hardly likely to be able to afford pocket money for the children or a winter jacket, school outings and nutritious meals during one and the same month. This is serious because a low living standard not only affects children's health but also their education and their subsequent development.

Poverty increased more among children of foreign extraction than among other children in the 1990s, and financial recovery was slower in these families than among the majority. Today, almost half of all children living in economic straits are of foreign extraction. Children in newly-arrived immigrant families have been particularly hard hit.

Ominously enough, child poverty in Sweden does not appear to be a temporary phenomenon, despite the fact that the Swedish economy is back on the tracks. When general welfare standards improve in a society that is becoming increasingly polarised, young teenagers may find it hard not to be able to afford branded clothing, for instance, or a mobile phone. The current increase in thefts among children of mobile phones in particular – a modern status symbol for the young – is not necessarily a matter of chance.

The child as consumer

Ever since the construction of the welfare society began, children in Sweden have been regarded as a vulnerable group requiring protection not only from the toil of the adult world but also from commercial interests. As Sweden's minister for democratic affairs once declared: "Children must have the right to protected zones".

As long as children are unable to grasp the purpose of advertising, the Swedish Consumer Council takes the view that directing it at the young is undemocratic. Children are not aware that they are being exposed to commercial pressure. Consequently, TV advertising for children under 12 is banned in Sweden – a ban that the country has sought to find acceptance for in the rest of the European Union.

The ban on this type of advertising is primarily due to the assumption that young children cannot distinguish between advertising and ordinary programme content and the belief that it is unfair to manipulate children. Sweden also prohibits the dispatch of direct mail advertising to children under 16, and also, partly with children in mind, alcohol and tobacco advertising in general.

Wide-ranging prohibition in the advertising field does not mean, however, that children in Sweden are not under considerable pressure to acquire the 'right' products. Children have become a major consumer group that cannot be ignored.

There is a consumerist undercurrent running through Swedish society to the effect that children have a right to up-to-date consumer products and that parents have an obligation to meet their wishes. Peer pressure is a powerful factor in this connection, as are the hidden marketing practices of commercial companies.

However much families' **economic circumstances** may vary, the differences in children's own personal finances, for example how much pocket money they receive, are not so great. This applies to material resources also. Just over half of 10 to 18-year-olds have their own television and over 40% own a mobile phone. This suggests that parents make every effort to ensure that their children do not lose out.

(Source: Swedish Level of Living Survey for Children (*Barn-LNU*) 2000)

The organisation **BRIS (Children's Rights in Society)** was founded in 1971 with the aim of improving conditions for children and young people and increasing respect for them. In 2001 almost 200,000 calls were made to the BRIS Children's Helpline. The average age of callers was 13. 72% were girls, 28% boys. The most common issues raised were bullying (18%); family conflicts (12%); love/relationship problems (11%); sexual development, sexuality and pregnancy (10%); physical abuse (6.9%) and sexual abuse (5.5%).

Find out more about BRIS at www.bris.se.

When things look hopeless – children and stress

Stress among children and young people has been identified as a problem in Sweden since the early 1990s. It was then that many children began phoning the emergency line run by the children's rights organisation BRIS because they were suffering from psychosomatic disorders. Many of them had stomachaches and headaches – and felt depressed and lacked faith in the future.

Children had fewer adults to discuss their problems with. Many school psychologists disappeared as a result of the cuts that occurred during the crisis years of the 1990s. The queues to child and youth guidance clinics grew – and still involve long waits. Meanwhile, noise levels have long been high in many schools and preschools. And the pace of family life has remained hectic, not least due to job pressure among parents.

Under the circumstances, it is perhaps not surprising that headaches and stomachaches are on the increase among Swedish children, and that stress is occurring at an increasingly early age. One child in three aged 10–18 reports having a headache, stomachache or sleep problems at least once a week. Many children feel sad or 'down' as well.

Doctors have raised the alarm and warned policy-makers to expect such consequences as depression, aggressiveness, overweight and premature cardio-vascular diseases in a generation of children who have paid a high price for the adult world's new-found insistence on efficiency.

Swedish courts nowadays base their rulings on what is best for the child as regards living arrangements, custody and access to his or her parents after **divorce**. A court may, for instance, refuse to revoke a decision on joint custody, as in most cases it is considered the best solution for the child. About 10% of all divorces in Sweden end up in court.

More than half of all children born in Sweden are born to **cohabiting** but not married parents.

After a divorce or separation, both parents are obliged to contribute to the costs of bringing up their children. In cases of shared custody it is the parent with whom the child chiefly lives who receives the money on behalf of the child. It is important to note that, unlike in many countries, **maintenance** is paid for the child rather than for the support of the ex-partner. In cases where a parent for one reason or another fails to make the agreed payments, the parent with whom the child lives may receive a maintenance advance for the child from the social insurance office to cover the shortfall.

Child-friendly divorce

When mothers and fathers go their separate ways – and they fairly often do in Sweden – children should not have to choose sides.

In Sweden, parents usually continue to share responsibility for the children after a divorce or a separation. Should one of the parents wish to terminate joint custody because they feel such an arrangement is harmful for the child, they must take their case to the local social services committee or to the local district court. To avoid the prospect of harrowing courtroom wrangles, parents can reach custody agreements with the social services committee.

Under Swedish law it is the best interests of the child – and not the parents' interests – that determine who is granted custody and how living arrangements and parental access are decided. A parent may only be deprived of custody if there are very strong reasons for such a course, such as evidence that the child has been exposed to sexual abuse or assault or is in danger of being abducted. When faced with a choice between protecting the child and supporting the child's right of access to his or her parents, courts are required to rule in favour of protection.

Is there such a thing as a child-friendly divorce? And if so, what form does it take? Researchers and experts are still not agreed on how divorces or separations should be arranged so as to be in the best interests of the child – at least not as regards the practicalities, such as the child's living arrangements.

One model that has been proposed involves the child remaining in the home and the mother and father moving in and out at regular intervals. Even if such a model may be fair from the child's viewpoint, it has not struck much of a chord with parents for practical reasons.

On the other hand, a growing number of children in Sweden have begun to live with their divorced parents alternately, for roughly equally long periods, often spending a week with mum and the following week with dad, and so on. For such an arrangement to succeed the child must, clearly, feel secure with both parents. It is important for the parents to go on living within a reasonable distance of each other and their relationship must be one of mutual respect.

In August 2002 just over 10,000 children aged 0 to 17 were registered as **asylum seekers** in Sweden. 437 of them had no guardian with them, although most either arrived with a relative or are now living with family members who were already in Sweden.

(Source: Swedish Migration Board)

Children in flight

Every year, several thousand children come to Sweden seeking asylum, most of them in the company of their families, but some unaccompanied. Virtually all of them harbour unpleasant memories – of war or fleeing danger. Many have travelled a very dangerous route to get to Sweden.

All children living in Sweden for the purpose of seeking asylum or a residence permit, or because they have been granted temporary refuge, are entitled to schooling in the public education system, whether at preschool, compulsory or upper secondary level. Such children are also entitled to medical care on the same terms as other children living in Sweden.

But there are also children who are kept hidden by their parents following a decision by the Swedish authorities to expel them. Under Swedish law, these children are not entitled to attend school but are entitled to healthcare.

Children in hiding have not chosen a life underground themselves, and they almost always end up in bad emotional shape as a result of their own and their parents' helplessness and the mental pressures involved.

Children's rights advocates argue that these children, for the sake of their psychological wellbeing, need to be offered the opportunity to attend school or preschool like other children, something to which a number of local authorities have now agreed.

Unaccompanied children seeking asylum are another group in a particularly vulnerable situation. They often have traumatic experiences and separations to plague their thoughts.

The situation of both unaccompanied and hidden refugee children has received a good deal of media attention in recent years. What is worrying the authorities is that refugee children who have come to Sweden on their own sometimes disappear from refugee reception centres and neither the police nor staff are able to determine their whereabouts. There are also alle-

gations that in some cases unaccompanied refugee children have been exploited in the child sex trade in Sweden.

Children's rights workers have declared that the plight of many children seeking refuge in Sweden must improve if the country wishes to fulfil its obligations under the UN Convention on the Rights of the Child.

Oda Lill and her secret garden

Oda Lill loves London and wants to live in Jamaica sometime. She wants to be a photographer or a film director. She never feels it's too much having four older brothers. She does sometimes find herself shouting at her parents though. Up in her red bedroom she plays the guitar and collects photos of people she doesn't know. On Saturday it's time for a party in her mum's art gallery.

Are you happy with your life?
I have a lot of fun and that, but it was more fun when I was little. Nowadays you have to think about your appearance. You have to make yourself up and get yourself ready. When you were young you could go into town in your pants.

How are you enjoying school?
I only have two good teachers. I don't like the other ones at my school. They're quite young and they try to ingratiate themselves with us and be like us.

Who can you talk to about everything?
My friend Hilda.

Is there anyone at your school you have to watch out for?
No, there isn't. But you hide from some of the best-looking guys so that you don't have to stand there red as a beetroot. There are no real thugs at my school, though.

Lund, in the southernmost province of Skåne, is an ancient university and cathedral city. It dates from around AD 990 and belonged to Denmark until 1658, when Skåne became Swedish. The university was founded in 1668, making it Sweden's second oldest after Uppsala (founded in 1477).

The day Oda came into the world, everything was so beautiful, says Oda's mother.

It was a glorious spring evening, the sky was high and clear and the air was warm from the sun. Outside the house, apple and plum trees blossomed and wild spring flowers bloomed.

Almost fourteen years later, on another day in May, Oda sits in her elder brother Bobo's blue couch in southern Sweden, where the landscape is flat as a pancake and airplanes cruise in to land over windmills and yellowy green fields of rape edged with red poppies.

"You could say I was born on a perfect day," says Oda.

In the intervening years, she has been named after the Norwegian painter and feminist Oda Krohg, learnt to play the guitar, and developed both a sense of humour and a taste for clothes.

Her friends, her brothers and music are now among the most important things in her life – a life spent in the small university town of Lund. Malmö, where all her brothers except Sami live, is just a quarter of an hour away by commuter train. Sami lives in London with Meredith, a photographer from Bermuda.

"I love London," says Oda.

Last year she flew there for a visit. It was the first time she travelled alone.

The lilac bushes have blossomed overnight, and sunlight is now streaming into the flat. In the hall, Oda has enveloped Bobo in a long, tumbling hug.

Four brothers are important people. Over the years, they have rocked Oda to sleep, admonished her, recommended records and wrestled with her.

"It's always fun talking to my brothers," she says.

"Of course they look after me! Bobo usually tells me I mustn't come home late and that I mustn't drink alcohol. Agge doesn't say it straight out in the same way....but he doesn't like me being out late, either."

The fact that Bobo, Miku and Sami are Oda's half-brothers while August, or Agge, is a full brother hasn't affected the way they feel about each other

in the slightest, says Oda. Their mother and the two fathers have always encouraged all the siblings to be together.

A few years ago, Miku, Oda's second eldest brother, developed a mental illness. Oda doesn't feel that her life has been affected to any great extent by it.

"OK, he's a bit more peculiar than he used to be, and he's a bit different. But he's still my brother and it makes no difference to me whether he's ill or not. I've got used to living with it – it's just the way he is."

When Oda began her fifth year at school, the Lill family moved further south in Skåne, to a house in one of the older parts of Lund. At first, Oda didn't want to move, but she now feels it would be better if her old friends from Ängelholm moved to Lund than if she moved back. There's more to do in Lund, more concerts to go to.

The new house has a studio for Oda's mother, Görel, who is an artist, a small gallery and two upstairs rooms set slightly apart that are Oda's. You reach them via a steep, narrow staircase.

The heart of the house is the small garden, which is invisible from the street and which is full of Görel's art and of clay pots, plants and garden furniture. It is also the home of Freya the cat, named after the ancient Nordic goddess of fertility.

Oda is happy here, but when she leaves school she wants to spend a year or two in Jamaica and then perhaps go to Atlantic College in Wales, where Sami studied.

If she stays in Sweden she'll live in Skåne, close to her friends and family.

"I'm looking forward to growing up and having a flat of my own, where I can do whatever I like and have more parties," says Oda.

Sharing a flat with Hilda, one of her very best friends, is, however, a must.

"Hilda and I are going to have lots of fun even if we don't have much money. I'd never dare live on my own. It would feel empty – I'm used to always having my family around me."

In fact she sometimes feels a bit alone in the new house, as there are no longer any brothers around to wrestle with.

Another thing that Oda is not too happy about is that it is difficult to meet her friends as often as she would like.

"I'm almost never with them," she says. "They often have to go into town, do homework or play handball, which is what one of my friends does. They haven't time to be with me. So I sit in my room quite a lot, playing the guitar, or I send mails or play around with Lunarstorm."

Almost all of Oda's friends have a page on the Lunarstorm site that people can write to.

Bobo's Norwegian wife, Annette, who is a psychologist at a refugee reception centre, arrives home. Bobo is going out to practise with his rowing club, and has to get ready. Oda is taking the train back to Lund.

Sami and Meredith are due in from London in a couple of days' time. Meredith is having an exhibition in Görel's gallery. Then perhaps there will be time for Oda and her brothers to get together on Sunday?

"Good, then we'll have a falafel and go and play boule in the park," says Bobo.

Oda is in a bad mood. The legs of her jeans are muddy and she is cold as she walks down Södra Esplanaden with her classmates. Her school wants to develop a heath profile, which has meant adding two health days to the syllabus this spring. The first begins with a massage, after which Oda and the other pupils go for a walk through Lund.

An April shower is drenching them.

"There's nothing wrong with health, but walking in the rain can't be very good for you," moans Agnes, one of Oda's classmates, when they return to school for a lesson in home economics: how to make a nutritious breakfast.

Almost all the girls in class 7d have tight, dark blue jeans and black tops. Julia, Disa, Maria and Oda are in the same group. Agnes, Sofia, Alice and Alexandra are in another.

It is not unusual for the girls in the class to keep to themselves and the boys to do the same.

"There are some girls' gangs and some boys' gangs," says Agnes.

"Ha!" snorts Daniel. "There're at least a hundred girls' gangs."

The pupils don't wait for everyone to be seated. Each group starts eating as soon as its 'breakfast' is ready. Ten girls are jammed in round Oda's table, enjoying one another's company.

"Some people say parents and children meet less and less nowadays, and that families don't have their meals together any more. How do you feel about that?" asks Annika, their home economics teacher.

"Our family never eat together," says someone.

"We always eat together," sighs Oda.

"There are those who claim that's why some pupils are so rowdy in school. But don't you think it's nice to eat as a family? I think you should have at least one meal a day together. Do you agree?" wonders Annika.

The class agrees.

They, too, eat one meal a day together – at school, where lunches are free. But does everyone in fact eat at school?

"Yes, mostly," says Julia. "But sometimes we go to the shop and buy food."

Previous page

New horizons. Behind Oda and Annika, the bridge to Denmark and the Continent. Oda wants to see the world yet still live near family and friends.

At their next lesson, they consider whether the school can do anything to improve pupils' health. The class are asked to fill out a questionnaire about things like whether they feel lonely, whether they smoke or take snuff and whether they sometimes eat in the school cafeteria.

"If you only smoke cross out 'snuff'," says Anna, one of the two class teachers. She is young and speaks with a mild, pleasant voice. On this particular day, there'll be no finger-wagging about smoking, perhaps so that the pupils feel free to answer the questions honestly.

"Someone's mobile is ringing. We've told you not to have your mobiles on."

The mobile stops ringing.

One suggestion for improving health is never to force the pupils to do homework. Another is to abolish maths.

"Are you serious – would you really prefer not to have maths?" the teacher asks.

A murmur ripples through the room.

"You shouldn't take everything we say seriously," someone replies.

"I have to take you seriously. It would be terrible if I didn't," says Anna.

New suggestions are offered. Air fresheners in the dressing rooms is one. More late mornings another. More nutrition in school food. More recreation rooms. Do more practical things during lessons. Wash cutlery properly. Outdoor school lunches in the summer.

"Quiet, please! One at a time," says Anna.

She is writing all the suggestions on the blackboard and it is taking time.

Oda has lowered her head onto the desk and she is whispering to Anna.

"Get rid of bad teachers and get better ones!" says Eric.

"Pupils have to put in a bit of effort, too, Eric!" says Daniel.

When some of the girls try to offer their suggestions and are drowned by the clamour, Anna gets angry:

"Listen, there are some girls here trying to say something!"

The pupils then get to vote for four suggestions each. Anna collects the voting slips.

"How about ending the lesson quietly by listening to what happened to Anja?" asks Anna.

The class agrees.

"Do you remember what happened last time? Anja lives in the basement at old Sergei's place and she works at the market. She's grown tougher now and begun to assert her rights," Anna says, recapitulating.

She reads from a Swedish book by Mecka Lind about a street child in Moscow.

Görel, Oda and Ivar. Friends – most of the time.

The class grow silent as the story describes how Anja receives an unexpected visit in her basement room one night. It's a drunken old man who says he wants to play cat and mouse with her. He tries to tear off her clothes.

Fortunately, the man's wife arrives to interrupt the proceedings.

Anja is unable to sleep all that night. She feels as repulsive as her assailant although it is not her fault that he tried to attack her.

The following morning, Anja leaves to beg at the underground station. She has nowhere to go. It is 9 May and the people of Moscow are celebrating the victory over Nazi Germany. During the day Anja saves an old alcoholic from being robbed by some young men in expensive tracksuits, and she finds a hiding-place of her own in thick shrubbery. She takes the old man there, too. That night, Anja sees a shower of stars in the heavens.

A promising friendship dawns.

At the café. Oda and her friends usually meet at someone's house – if there isn't a concert to go to, that is. Music and her brothers are the most important things in Oda's life just now.

A black wooden entrance leads in to a semi-concealed garden, Oda's garden. School is over and up on a flat roof sit Oda, Disa and Anna. They swing their jeans-clad legs as they sit there at a safe distance from the cobblestone street. Below them, people hurry to and fro in the spring warmth.

Oda and her friends spend the afternoon trying to guess the names of unknown passers-by.

"Marcus! Is your name Marcus?"

It's Oda Lill who asks. She calls to one of the men passing below.

"No," replies the man, a little hesitantly, as if somewhat embarrassed by all this attention from on high.

"Oh, look, there he is! A genuine Åke!" cries Disa, and it sounds as though she has been yearning for an Åke all her life.

But Åke disappears round the corner without reacting.

On the same roof as Oda, Disa and Anna, two men in blue overalls are working.

The rain has leaked into Görel's studio and the men have just finished repairing the roof. They pull the dark green tarpaulin away from the big skylights.

Instantly, badly-needed light fills the studio below, where a children's art session is in progress. Today, the group is listening to music – a classical, romantic work. Around the walls, the pupils stand in their painting clothes daubing white sheets of paper. They are given advice and encouragement by Görel, who is also operating the stereo.

Out in the garden, Freya prowls. She has detected what appears to be a mouse in the ivy.

The bell on the gate rings as the door opens. It must be Oda's father, Ivar, on his way home from the office. Ivar walks rapidly up the wooden stairs, but pauses and asks one of the men if he has time to come down for a talk. Ivar will soon be off to a new meeting and has very, very little time. He is a self-employed consultant and is almost always in a hurry.

In the paved garden, the peonies are blooming, clearly visible from the kitchen, where Oda goes to make tea for her friends.

Oda does not go out to cafés much nowadays, unlike last year.

"I don't know how much money I spent," she says.

So she now prefers to meet her friends at someone's home.

When she goes out in the evenings, to the disco or a concert, her parents have decided she should usually be home by half past twelve. It depends a little on what time her friends have to be in by.

Oda is allowed to decide quite a lot of things for herself. Her parents sometimes agree, for instance, to pay for clothes that they are not keen on, that they think look simply shabby. Oda has also been to the Hultsfred rock music festival two years running – something that many fourteen-year-olds can only dream of doing.

"This year, I'm going to the Roskilde festival in Denmark."

But Oda doesn't decide everything.

"It works like this: first, I decide, then mum comes along. She says something like, no, that doesn't look good, I think it needs changing a bit. For example, I chose dark red and dark blue for my walls. They ended up dark red and a sort of turquoise colour," says Oda.

"So it's freedom under responsibility. But I'm glad she didn't decide exactly how the room should look. It's my room, after all."

It's going to be another warm evening, and it's still light outside although it's eight in the evening. Nature is awakening – and people are, too. They soak up the sun by the university, along the cathedral walls and in the city park. In the main square, all the benches are occupied by young people eating ice cream.

Tomorrow is the last day of April, Walpurgis Night. By tradition, May bonfires will be lit all over Sweden. In the old days, this was to frighten off witches and dangerous animals before cows and sheep were released into their summer pastures. Outside the white university building in Lund, the students will celebrate by taking off their white graduation caps and singing traditional choral songs about winter having spent its rage.

Oda's friends have other plans. A funfair is under construction in the city park and some of them are going there. But Oda has decided to take things easy and stay home. Meredith and Sami are on their way, and on Saturday the exhibition will open and the whole family will be able to meet.

Even if becoming an adult is an attractive prospect, it's not so bad being a fourteen-year-old, says Oda.

"I have a lot of fun with Hilda and Sarah and my other friends. So in a way, I'd just like to go on being fourteen."

A place of one's own

Children must be able to feel free and play freely – this is the reasoning behind the efforts being made in Sweden to give children their own public space. Children need a place in the world – their own territory and an environment they can live and feel happy in.

They need playgrounds that present a challenge – but not dangers. Children learn about the world around them through their senses, through their body and movement. And they are affected by their surroundings, both outdoors and indoors. Ellen Key understood this over a century ago.

For many years, the design of playgrounds in Sweden was a subject of fairly detailed government instructions. Today, local authorities assume a greater responsibility for this. The Education Act requires school premises to be "suited to their purpose". New European standards for play equipment now apply and there is also a Planning and Building Act that regulates outdoor environments. In addition, the Swedish Product Safety Act extends to play equipment used in public spaces.

Research shows that children who play outdoors are less often sick. Outdoor play helps children to unwind and loosen up – they play whatever they like. They decide their own activities with less interference from adults. Their concentration and balance improve. Bearing in mind that Swedish children have become increasingly overweight in recent years, all this is of course a welcome side effect of children having fun.

Architects nowadays are well aware that their work impacts on children's daily lives. Architects – or municipal decision-makers – who consult with children and view the playground or yard from the child's perspective, now understand the importance of creating secure environments close to the adults and slightly more 'dangerous' ones further off.

The child's perspective is to be given special consideration in the plan-

Sweden (with 5.2 deaths per 100,000 children per annum) ranks number one, followed by the UK, Italy and the Netherlands, according to **UNICEF's League Table of Child Deaths by Injury in Rich Nations** (Feb 2001, Innocenti Research Centre, Florence). At least 12,000 child deaths a year could be prevented if all OECD countries had the same child injury death rate as Sweden.

Sweden has countless lakes, rivers and coastal waters in which to bathe, and for many children summer holidays mean the chance to go swimming. **Swimming lessons** have long been the responsibility of schools. All children in Sweden are supposed to be able to swim 200 metres and cope with emergencies in and beside water by the age of twelve. But a growing number of schools have less and less swimming on the syllabus. Nowadays, those parents in a position to do so send their children to municipal swimming classes outside school hours.

ning of roads and transport. For the planners, this is a challenge, not least in view of the steady growth of motor traffic in Sweden. Motor traffic is a threat to children and restricts their freedom of movement. The National Road Administration, however, is among the Swedish government agencies that have progressed furthest both in the use of child impact analyses and in the importance they attach to children's views.

Thinking on child safety has progressed in Sweden considerably as a result of collaboration between interested parties in many different areas, from nappy-changing tables and lifejackets to baby comforters and road safety.

Land of a thousand tales – children and culture

It is sometimes said that childhood was better in the old days, as children in modern Sweden have to contend with a chaotic and often indecipherable flow of information from the media. They are no longer free to remain 'children'. They are inundated with soap operas, commercial advertising, scenes of violence and sexualised messages from the adult world. Via the media, children are introduced at an early age into a complicated adult world and partake of events that they themselves have not yet experienced and cannot reasonably be expected to.

The nursery tales of old may have been cruel, but they were about princesses and enchanted animals, not about ordinary people. Perhaps those stories were more conducive to a child's development than today's flood of media messages.

It is difficult to believe, however, that the children of times past were less exposed to evils and abominations. In agrarian Sweden, before the end of the 19th century, childhood was singularly brief for the great majority of children, who were forced to toil from an early age in very tough circumstances. Only the children of the bourgeoisie were privileged to experience what became the romanticised picture of childhood at that time – childhood as a period of idyllic innocence lived out behind white-painted gates.

Children's situations have of course differed throughout history depending on the individual's social class and cultural frame of reference. But if Swedish children's culture until recently comprised a treasure chest of films, plays and books common to all, it has been replaced by a widely disparate culture, thanks to generations of immigrants from a large number of countries. Many children in Sweden today fall asleep to the sound of Persian or Arabic folk tales and not necessarily to stories about Alfie Atkins or Karlsson-on-the Roof.

A survey carried out by the National Council for Cultural Affairs in 1999 revealed that 67% of parents with young children **read aloud to their children** every day. After a number of nationwide activities and campaigns a new survey in 2001 found that the figure had risen to 70%.

The fact that Sweden is developing into a multicultural society does not mean, though, that children are not acquiring a common frame of reference. The stories of Astrid Lindgren, for instance, are popular with most children. She, if anyone, understood children's spiritual needs and took young people seriously. Her stories contain not only excitement and a passion for living, as in the books about Pippi and Mardie. They also contain dark swathes of death, evil and the cruelty of life, as in the books about the Brothers Lionheart.

It is precisely this that may perhaps symbolise Swedish children's culture – the conviction that you can talk to children about anything, however difficult, as long as you do so in a language they understand. Children's stories do not always need to be edifying. Children can listen to tales of alcoholism, mental illness and divorce, but they must never be left without hope.

About a century ago, the legendary Swedish children's author Elsa Beskow was among the first to adopt a children's perspective in her books. A few decades later, Astrid Lindgren came out even more strongly on the side of the child. In Astrid Lindgren's world, children were entitled to their games, their opinions and their freedom – several decades before the adoption of the UN Child Convention.

As early as the mid-1940s, when publishing her first book about a certain controversial young lady with protruding red plaits, she seems to have made clear that children's opinions are to be reckoned with in the same way as adult's opinions. No one can make decisions over the head of the strongest girl in the world simply because they're a grownup. You have to convince Pippi Longstocking that the decision is a good and wise one.

The fact that children in Sweden are often considered independent and inquisitive is sometimes said to be due to Astrid Lindgren – she and Pippi Longstocking raised Swedish children to be sceptical of authority.

Equally, erring adults can expect little mercy from the pen of Astrid Lindgren. Adults are never entitled to let children down – however difficult their own circumstances may be.

In Sweden, it is felt that bringing children into contact with the imagination via storytelling and reading is so crucial to their development that parents who visit the child health care centre for the first time after the birth are often given a children's book as a gift.

Public libraries also try to coax children into reading, learning and expressing themselves by providing story readings, school programmes and mobile library visits. Special government grants are available for making museums more child-friendly, while programmes produced by public service TV are required to maintain very high standards across the board.

A relatively new development is the emphasis on culture produced by children themselves. The adult world has woken up to the fact that children are not only consumers of culture but also producers. And children's creative output deserves respect.

Ultimately, Swedish cultural policy aims to provide children with the means and ability to express themselves on as equal terms as possible. Those who work with children, however, often take the view that the fun they have – feeling, thinking and expressing themselves – is valuable in itself. In this day and age, childhood is after all no longer simply a preparation for adult life. It is also an ongoing process under way right now, and it must be made the most of.

Forever young

In one sense, childhood has been prolonged in recent decades because young people have been entering working life increasingly late. In another sense, childhood has been curtailed, as children often play a central part in modern Swedish families and are expected to take a range of decisions themselves. It is indeed sometimes claimed that the family's power centre has shifted from the father to the offspring.

Families are relatively small in Sweden – grandparents tend to lead their own lives, often far away from their children. Without a granny – often a central figure for children in other countries – life can sometimes be lonely for Swedish children.

The urban, well-to-do middle classes in Sweden, however, are expected to ensure that their children engage in 'stimulating' and 'useful' activities. Accordingly, their children's leisure time is filled with activity – sometimes, apparently, to such an extent that there isn't much time left for leisure.

Other children, probably a majority, are allowed just 'to exist' to a greater extent. Their parents accept that they have neither the time nor the money to keep their children constantly occupied. And the children – hopefully – then have the time and space to play in peace and quiet, and to develop their imagination.

Swedes tend to view the ideal childhood as one that lasts for as long as possible. Children have 'the right to a childhood', rich in relationships and experiences. Childhood must have room for nature, for flights of fancy and for stories. And children are entitled to adults' time.

In practice, however, childhood is inevitably neither perfect nor an endless adventure. In recent years, childhood has in a sense become shorter as a result of the sexualisation of children by the fashion and entertainment industries. Young children still in their preschool years, especially girls, aspire to be, if not adults, at least teenagers. We may not have progressed as far as we might imagine from the historical image of children as 'little adults'.

The author. Tiina Meri is a journalist, born in Sweden in 1972. She has been a leader writer on *Dagens Nyheter*, Sweden's biggest morning newspaper, and has also worked as a freelance journalist in Tallinn, Estonia.

The photographer. Maria Söderberg was born in 1959 and grew up in Arjeplog, Norrbotten, in northernmost Sweden. She is a documentary photographer and has worked extensively in countries such as Afghanistan, India and Belarus.